CONT

D0196184

SUPER
SPEEDY CHICKEN

QUICK HOT AND SOUR CHICKEN SOUP

- 2 cups water
- 2 cups chicken broth
- 1 package (about 10 ounces) refrigerated fully cooked chicken breast strips, cut into pieces
- 1 package (about 7 ounces) chicken-flavored rice and vermicelli mix
- 1 jalapeño pepper, minced
- 2 green onions, chopped
- 1 tablespoon soy sauce
- 1 tablespoon lime juice
- 1 tablespoon minced fresh cilantro

1. Combine water, broth, chicken, rice mix, jalapeño, green onions and soy sauce in large saucepan; bring to a boil over high heat. Reduce heat to low; cover and simmer 20 minutes or until rice is tender, stirring occasionally.

2. Stir in lime juice; sprinkle with cilantro.

Makes 4 servings

CREAMY TUSCAN BEAN & CHICKEN SOUP

2 cans (10¾ ounces **each**) CAMPBELL'S® Condensed Cream of Celery Soup (Regular **or** 98% Fat Free)

2 cups water

1 can (about 15 ounces) white kidney beans (cannellini), rinsed and drained

1 can (about 14½ ounces) diced tomatoes, undrained

2 cups shredded **or** diced cooked chicken

¼ cup bacon bits

3 ounces fresh baby spinach leaves (about 3 cups)

Olive oil

Grated Parmesan cheese

1. Heat the soup, water, beans, tomatoes, chicken and bacon in a 3-quart saucepan over medium-high heat to a boil.

2. Stir in the spinach. Cook for 5 minutes or until the spinach is wilted. Serve the soup with a drizzle of oil and sprinkle with the cheese.

Makes 4 servings

KITCHEN TIP: For the shredded chicken, purchase a rotisserie chicken. Remove the skin and bones. You can either shred the chicken with your fingers or use 2 forks.

PREP TIME: 10 minutes
COOK TIME: 10 minutes
TOTAL TIME: 20 minutes

CHICKEN TORTELLINI SOUP

- 6 cups chicken broth
- 1 package (9 ounces) refrigerated cheese and spinach tortellini
- 1 package (about 6 ounces) refrigerated fully cooked chicken breast strips, cut into bite-size pieces
- 2 cups baby spinach
- 4 to 6 tablespoons grated Parmesan cheese
- 1 tablespoon chopped fresh chives *or* 2 tablespoons sliced green onion

1. Bring broth to a boil in large saucepan over high heat. Add tortellini; cook over medium heat 5 minutes.

2. Stir in chicken and spinach. Reduce heat to low; cook 3 minutes or until chicken is heated through.

3. Sprinkle with Parmesan and chives.

Makes 4 servings

Spicy Thai Coconut Soup

3   cups coarsely shredded cooked chicken
     (about 12 ounces)
2   cups chicken broth
1   can (15 ounces) straw mushrooms, drained
1   can (about 14 ounces) light coconut milk
1   can (8 ounces) baby corn, drained
1   tablespoon minced fresh ginger
½   to 1 teaspoon red curry paste
2   tablespoons lime juice
¼   cup chopped fresh cilantro

1. Combine chicken, broth, mushrooms, coconut milk, corn, ginger and red curry paste in large saucepan; bring to a simmer over medium heat. Cook until heated through.

2. Stir in lime juice; sprinkle with cilantro.

Makes 4 servings

NOTE: Red curry paste can be found in jars in the Asian aisle of large grocery stores. Spice levels can vary between brands. Start with ½ teaspoon, then add more as desired.

MIDDLE EASTERN CHICKEN SOUP

2½ cups water

1 can (about 14 ounces) reduced-sodium chicken broth

1 can (about 15 ounces) chickpeas, rinsed and drained

1 cup chopped cooked chicken

1 small onion, chopped

1 carrot, chopped

1 clove garlic, minced

1 teaspoon dried oregano

1 teaspoon ground cumin

½ (10-ounce) package fresh spinach, stemmed and coarsely chopped

⅛ teaspoon black pepper

1. Combine water, broth, chickpeas, chicken, onion, carrot, garlic, oregano and cumin in large saucepan; bring to a boil over high heat. Reduce heat to medium-low; cover and simmer 15 minutes.

2. Stir in spinach and pepper; simmer, uncovered, 2 minutes or until spinach is wilted.

Makes 4 servings

Chunky Chicken Soup

1 tablespoon olive oil

1 onion, chopped

1 can (about 14 ounces) diced tomatoes

1 cup chicken broth

1 cup thinly sliced carrots

¼ teaspoon salt

⅛ teaspoon black pepper

3 cups sliced kale or baby spinach

1 cup diced cooked chicken breast

1. Heat oil in large saucepan over medium-high heat. Add onion; cook and stir about 5 minutes or until golden brown. Stir in tomatoes, broth, carrots, salt and pepper; bring to a boil. Reduce heat to medium-low; simmer about 10 minutes or until carrots are tender.

2. Stir in kale and chicken; cook about 4 minutes or until kale is wilted.

Makes 2 servings

ONE-POT
BEEF & PORK

QUICK AND ZESTY VEGETABLE SOUP

> 1 pound lean ground beef
> ½ cup chopped onion
> Salt and pepper
> 2 cans (14.5 ounces each) DEL MONTE® Italian Recipe Stewed Tomatoes
> 2 cans (14 ounces each) beef broth
> 1 can (14.5 ounces) DEL MONTE® Mixed Vegetables
> ½ cup uncooked medium egg noodles
> ½ teaspoon dried oregano

1. Brown meat with onion in large saucepan. Cook until onion is tender; drain. Season to taste with salt and pepper.

2. Stir in remaining ingredients. Bring to boil; reduce heat.

3. Cover and simmer 15 minutes or until noodles are tender.

Makes 8 servings

PREP TIME: 5 minutes
COOK TIME: 15 minutes

KIELBASA & CABBAGE SOUP

1 pound Polish kielbasa, cut into ½-inch cubes

1 package (16 ounces) coleslaw mix (shredded
green cabbage and carrots)

3 cans (14½ ounces each) beef broth

1 can (12 ounces) beer or nonalcoholic malt beverage

1 cup water

½ teaspoon caraway seeds

2 cups FRENCH'S® French Fried Onions, divided

Garnish: fresh dill sprigs (optional)

1. Coat 5-quart pot or Dutch oven with nonstick cooking spray.
Cook kielbasa over medium-high heat about 5 minutes or until
browned. Add coleslaw mix; sauté until tender.

2. Add broth, beer, water, caraway seeds and *1 cup* French Fried
Onions; bring to a boil over medium-high heat. Reduce heat to
low. Simmer, uncovered, 10 minutes to blend flavors. Spoon
soup into serving bowls; top with remaining onions. Garnish
with fresh dill sprigs, if desired.

Makes 8 servings

PREP TIME: 10 minutes
COOK TIME: 20 minutes

Quick and Easy Meatball Soup

2 cans (about 14 ounces each) Italian-style stewed tomatoes

2 cans (about 14 ounces each) beef broth

1 can (about 14 ounces) mixed vegetables

½ cup uncooked rotini pasta or small macaroni

½ teaspoon dried oregano

1 package (15 to 18 ounces) frozen Italian sausage meatballs without sauce, thawed

1. Combine tomatoes, broth, mixed vegetables, pasta and oregano in large saucepan.

2. Stir in meatballs; bring to a boil over medium-high heat. Reduce heat to medium-low; cover and simmer 15 minutes or until pasta is tender.

Makes 4 to 6 servings

MEDITERRANEAN BEAN AND SAUSAGE SOUP

½ pound sweet Italian pork sausage, casings removed

1 large onion, chopped

½ teaspoon garlic powder **or** 4 cloves garlic, minced

2 cups PREGO® Traditional Italian Sauce **or** Tomato, Basil & Garlic Italian Sauce

1¾ cups SWANSON® Chicken Broth (Regular, Natural Goodness® **or** Certified Organic)

1 can (about 15 ounces) black beans **or** pinto beans

1 can (about 15 ounces) white kidney beans (cannellini), drained

1 can (about 15 ounces) red kidney beans, drained

1. Cook sausage, onion and garlic powder in saucepan over medium-high heat until sausage is browned, stirring to separate the meat. Pour off any fat.

2. Add Italian sauce and broth and heat to a boil. Reduce heat to low and cook 10 minutes. Add beans and heat through.

Makes 4 servings

PREP TIME: 10 minutes
COOK TIME: 25 minutes
TOTAL TIME: 35 minutes

Sweet Potato and Ham Soup

1 tablespoon butter

1 leek, sliced

1 clove garlic, minced

4 cups reduced-sodium chicken broth

2 sweet potatoes, peeled and cut into ¾-inch pieces

½ pound ham, cut into ½-inch pieces

½ teaspoon dried thyme

2 ounces stemmed spinach, coarsely chopped

1. Melt butter in large saucepan over medium heat. Add leek and garlic; cook and stir until tender.

2. Add broth, sweet potatoes, ham and thyme; bring to a boil over high heat. Reduce heat to low; simmer 10 minutes or until sweet potatoes are tender.

3. Stir in spinach; simmer 2 minutes or until spinach is wilted. Serve immediately.

Makes 6 servings

SEAFOOD
IN A SNAP

ITALIAN FISH SOUP

  1 cup meatless pasta sauce

  ¾ cup water

  ¾ cup reduced-sodium chicken broth

  1 teaspoon Italian seasoning

  ¾ cup uncooked small pasta shells

1½ cups frozen vegetable blend, such as broccoli, carrots and water chestnuts or broccoli, carrots and cauliflower

  4 ounces fresh halibut or haddock steak, 1 inch thick, skinned and cut into 1-inch pieces

1. Combine pasta sauce, water, broth and Italian seasoning in medium saucepan; bring to a boil over high heat. Stir in pasta; return to a boil. Reduce heat to medium-low; cover and simmer 5 minutes.

2. Stir in vegetables and fish; return to a boil. Cover and simmer over medium-low heat 4 to 5 minutes or until pasta is tender and fish begins to flake when tested with fork.

Makes 2 servings

SAVORY SEAFOOD SOUP

2½ cups water or chicken broth
1½ cups dry white wine
1 onion, chopped
½ red bell pepper, chopped
½ green bell pepper, chopped
1 clove garlic, minced
8 ounces halibut, cut into 1-inch pieces
8 ounces sea scallops, cut into halves
1 teaspoon dried thyme
Juice of ½ lime
Dash hot pepper sauce
Salt and black pepper

1. Combine water, wine, onion, bell peppers and garlic in large saucepan; bring to a boil over high heat. Reduce heat to medium-low; cover and simmer 15 minutes or until bell peppers are tender, stirring occasionally.

2. Add fish, scallops and thyme; cook 2 minutes or until fish and scallops turn opaque.

3. Stir in lime juice and hot pepper sauce; season with salt and black pepper.

Makes 4 servings

TIP: If halibut is not available, substitute cod, ocean perch or haddock.

NEW ORLEANS FISH SOUP

1 can (about 15 ounces) cannellini beans, rinsed and
   drained

1 can (about 14 ounces) reduced-sodium chicken broth

1 yellow squash, halved lengthwise and sliced (1 cup)

1 tablespoon Cajun seasoning

2 cans (about 14 ounces each) stewed tomatoes

1 pound skinless firm fish fillets, such as grouper, cod
   or haddock, cut into 1-inch pieces

½ cup sliced green onions

1 teaspoon grated orange peel

1. Combine beans, broth, squash and Cajun seasoning in large
saucepan; bring to a boil over high heat.

2. Stir in tomatoes and fish; cover and simmer over medium-low
heat 3 to 5 minutes or until fish begins to flake when tested with
fork.

3. Stir in green onions and orange peel.

Makes 4 servings

SHRIMP & CORN CHOWDER WITH SUN-DRIED TOMATOES

1   can (10¾ ounces) CAMPBELL'S® Condensed
    Cream of Potato Soup

1½ cups half-and-half

2   cups whole kernel corn, drained

2   tablespoons sun-dried tomatoes, cut into strips

1   cup small **or** medium peeled and deveined cooked
    shrimp

2   tablespoons chopped fresh chives
    Ground black pepper

1. Heat the soup, half-and-half, corn and tomatoes in a 3-quart saucepan over medium heat to a boil. Reduce the heat to low. Cook for 10 minutes.

2. Stir in the shrimp and chives and cook until the mixture is hot and bubbling. Season with the black pepper.

Makes 4 servings

KITCHEN TIP: For a lighter version, use skim milk instead of the half-and-half.

PREP TIME: 10 minutes
COOK TIME: 20 minutes
TOTAL TIME: 30 minutes

NO-FUSS
VEGETABLES

SALSA GAZPACHO

1 jar (16 ounces) ORTEGA® Thick & Chunky Salsa

1½ cups water

1 cup finely chopped celery

1 cup peeled diced cucumber

½ cup finely chopped green bell pepper

½ cup finely chopped red bell pepper

¼ cup chopped green onion

1 can (4 ounces) ORTEGA® Diced Green Chiles

½ teaspoon POLANER® Minced Garlic

Salt and black pepper, to taste

¼ cup chopped fresh cilantro (optional)

1 cup croutons (optional)

COMBINE salsa, water, celery, cucumber, bell peppers, green onion, chiles, garlic and salt and pepper to taste in large bowl; mix well.

COVER and refrigerate 2 hours. If desired, top with cilantro and croutons before serving.

Makes 6 servings

EASY MUSHROOM SOUP

1¾ cups SWANSON® 50% Less Sodium Beef Broth
1¾ cups SWANSON® Natural Goodness® Chicken Broth
⅛ teaspoon ground black pepper
⅛ teaspoon dried rosemary leaves, crushed
2 cups sliced fresh mushrooms (about 8 ounces)
¼ cup thinly sliced carrot
¼ cup finely chopped onion
¼ cup sliced celery
¼ cup fresh **or** frozen peas
1 tablespoon sliced green onion

1. Heat the beef broth, chicken broth, black pepper, rosemary, mushrooms, carrot, onion, celery and peas in a 4-quart saucepan over medium heat to a boil. Reduce the heat to low. Cover and cook for 15 minutes.

2. Add the green onion. Cook for 5 minutes or until the vegetables are tender.

Makes 4 servings

PREP TIME: 15 minutes
COOK TIME: 25 minutes
TOTAL TIME: 40 minutes

Szechuan Vegetable Soup

2 cans (about 14 ounces each) vegetable broth

2 teaspoons minced garlic

1 teaspoon minced fresh ginger

¼ teaspoon red pepper flakes

1 package (16 ounces) frozen vegetable medley, such as broccoli, carrots, water chestnuts and red bell peppers

2 packages (3 ounces each) ramen noodles, any flavor,* or 5 ounces uncooked angel hair pasta, broken in half

3 tablespoons soy sauce

1 tablespoon dark sesame oil

¼ cup thinly sliced green onions

Discard seasoning packets.

1. Combine broth, garlic, ginger and red pepper flakes in large saucepan; bring to a boil over high heat. Add vegetables and noodles; cover and return to a boil. Reduce heat to medium-low; simmer, uncovered, 5 to 6 minutes or until vegetables and noodles are tender, stirring occasionally.

2. Stir in soy sauce and sesame oil; cook 3 minutes. Stir in green onions just before serving.

Makes 4 servings

NOTE: For a heartier, protein-packed main dish, add 1 package (14 ounces) extra firm tofu, drained and cut into ¾-inch cubes, to the broth mixture with the soy sauce and sesame oil.

PESTO AND TORTELLINI SOUP

   3 cans (about 14 ounces each) vegetable or chicken broth

   1 package (9 ounces) refrigerated cheese tortellini

   3 to 4 cups packed stemmed fresh spinach

   1 jar (7 ounces) roasted red peppers, drained and
       thinly sliced

   ¾ cup frozen green peas

   1 to 2 tablespoons prepared pesto

       Grated Parmesan cheese

1. Bring broth to a boil in large saucepan over high heat.
Add tortellini; return to a boil. Reduce heat to medium;
simmer 6 minutes.

2. Stir in spinach, roasted peppers, peas and pesto; simmer
2 minutes or until pasta is tender. Serve with Parmesan.

Makes 6 servings

ITALIAN TOMATO AND PASTA SOUP

  5 cups water
  2 tablespoons dried vegetable flakes, soup greens
      or dehydrated vegetables
  1 tablespoon minced onion
  1 teaspoon sugar
  1 teaspoon chicken bouillon granules
  1 teaspoon Italian seasoning
  ½ teaspoon minced garlic
  ¼ teaspoon black pepper
  1 can (about 28 ounces) crushed tomatoes
  3 cups chopped fresh spinach
  2½ cups uncooked farfalle (bowtie) or rotini pasta
  4 to 6 slices bacon, crisp-cooked and crumbled (optional)
  ½ cup grated Parmesan cheese

1. Combine water, vegetable flakes, onion, sugar, bouillon, Italian seasoning, garlic and pepper in large saucepan; bring to a boil over medium-high heat. Boil 10 to 12 minutes.

2. Stir in tomatoes, spinach, pasta and bacon, if desired; cook over medium heat 10 to 12 minutes or until pasta is tender. Sprinkle with Parmesan.

Makes 4 servings

HEARTY
BEANS

MINESTRONE SOUP

2 cans (about 14 ounces each) vegetable broth

1 can (28 ounces) crushed tomatoes in tomato purée

1 can (about 15 ounces) cannellini beans, rinsed and drained

¾ cup uncooked small shell pasta

1 package (16 ounces) frozen vegetable medley, such as broccoli, green beans, carrots and red peppers

4 to 6 teaspoons prepared pesto

1. Combine broth, tomatoes and beans in large saucepan; bring to a boil over high heat. Stir in pasta; cook 7 minutes.

2. Stir in vegetables; cook until pasta is tender and vegetables are heated through.

3. Spoon about 1 teaspoon pesto in center of each serving.

Makes 4 to 6 servings

PICANTE BLACK BEAN SOUP

- 1 tablespoon reserved bacon drippings* or olive oil
- 1 large onion, chopped
- 1 clove garlic, minced
- 2 cans (15 ounces each) black beans, undrained
- 1 can (about 14 ounces) beef broth
- 1¼ cups water
- ¾ cup picante sauce, plus additional for serving
- ½ teaspoon salt
- ½ teaspoon dried oregano
- 4 slices bacon, crisp-cooked and coarsely chopped*

  Sour cream

When cooking bacon, reserve drippings to use for cooking onion and garlic.

1. Heat bacon drippings in large saucepan over medium-high heat. Add onion and garlic; cook and stir 3 minutes.

2. Stir in beans with liquid, broth, water, ¾ cup picante sauce, salt and oregano. Reduce heat to low; cover and simmer 20 minutes.

3. Sprinkle with bacon; serve with sour cream and additional picante sauce.

Makes 6 to 8 servings

QUICK TUSCAN BEAN, TOMATO AND SPINACH SOUP

2 cans (about 14 ounces each) diced tomatoes with onions

1 can (about 14 ounces) reduced-sodium chicken broth

2 teaspoons sugar

2 teaspoons dried basil

¾ teaspoon Worcestershire sauce

1 can (about 15 ounces) cannellini beans, rinsed and drained

3 ounces fresh baby spinach

1 tablespoon extra virgin olive oil

1. Combine tomatoes, broth, sugar, basil and Worcestershire sauce in large saucepan; bring to a boil over high heat. Reduce heat to low; simmer 10 minutes.

2. Stir in beans and spinach; cook 5 minutes or until spinach is tender.

3. Stir in oil just before serving.

Makes 4 servings

Black and White Mexican Bean Soup

1 tablespoon vegetable oil

1 cup chopped onion

½ teaspoon POLANER® Minced Garlic

¼ cup all-purpose flour

1 packet (1.25 ounces) ORTEGA® Taco Seasoning Mix

2 cups milk

1 can (about 14 ounces) chicken broth

1 package (16 ounces) frozen corn

1 can (15 ounces) JOAN OF ARC® Great Northern Beans, rinsed, drained

1 can (15 ounces) ORTEGA® Black Beans, rinsed, drained

1 can (4 ounces) ORTEGA® Fire-Roasted Diced Green Chiles

2 tablespoons chopped fresh cilantro

HEAT oil in large pan or Dutch oven over medium-high heat. Add onion and garlic; cook and stir 4 to 5 minutes or until onion is tender.

STIR in flour and seasoning mix; gradually stir in milk until blended.

ADD broth, corn, beans, and green chiles; stir well. Bring to a boil, stirring constantly. Reduce heat to low; simmer 15 minutes or until thickened, stirring occasionally.

STIR in cilantro. Serve warm.

Makes 6 servings

Pasta Fagioli

- 1 jar (1 pound 8 ounces) RAGÚ® Chunky Pasta Sauce
- 1 can (19 ounces) white kidney beans, rinsed and drained
- 1 package (10 ounces) frozen chopped spinach, thawed
- 8 ounces ditalini pasta, cooked and drained (reserve 2 cups pasta water)

1. Combine Pasta Sauce, beans, spinach, pasta and reserved pasta water in 6-quart saucepan; heat through.

2. Season, if desired, with salt, ground black pepper and grated Parmesan cheese.

Makes 4 servings

PREP TIME: 20 minutes
COOK TIME: 10 minutes

CONTENTS

DELICIOUSLY
SIMPLE SKILLETS

SWIRLY NOODLE TACO SKILLET

- 1 pound ground beef
- 1 onion, diced (about 1 cup)
- 1 packet (1.25 ounces) ORTEGA® Taco Seasoning Mix
- 1 can (7 ounces) ORTEGA® Fire-Roasted Diced Green Chiles
- 1 jar (16 ounces) ORTEGA® Salsa, any variety
- ½ pound rotini or fusilli pasta, uncooked
- Shredded Cheddar cheese (optional)

BROWN ground beef and onion in large skillet over medium-high heat 6 to 8 minutes, stirring to break up meat. Drain fat.

ADD taco seasoning mix, chiles, salsa and 2 cups water; stir to combine. Add pasta and stir. Reduce heat to low. Cover and cook 12 to 14 minutes or until pasta is cooked through. Serve with cheese.

Makes 6 servings

TIP: This dish also makes a great taco filling for ORTEGA® Yellow Corn Taco Shells or soft flour tortillas.

CHICKEN COUSCOUS

1 tablespoon olive oil

8 ounces boneless skinless chicken breasts, cut into
  1-inch pieces

4 medium zucchini, sliced

1 can (about 14 ounces) diced tomatoes

1 can (about 14 ounces) reduced-sodium chicken broth

1 teaspoon Italian seasoning

1 cup uncooked whole wheat couscous

1. Heat oil in large skillet over medium-high heat. Add chicken;
cook and stir 4 minutes or until lightly browned.

2. Add zucchini, tomatoes, broth and Italian seasoning; simmer
over low heat 15 minutes, stirring occasionally.

3. Remove from heat. Stir in couscous; cover and let stand
7 minutes. Fluff with fork.

Makes 4 servings

Southwestern Turkey Stew

1 tablespoon vegetable oil

1 small onion, finely chopped

1 clove garlic, minced

2 cups reduced-sodium chicken broth

2 cups smoked turkey breast, cut into ½-inch pieces

2 cups frozen corn

1 can (about 14 ounces) diced tomatoes

1 package (about 8 ounces) red beans and rice mix

1 to 2 canned chipotle peppers in adobo sauce, drained and minced

Chopped green onion (optional)

1. Heat oil in large skillet over medium-high heat. Add onion and garlic; cook and stir 3 minutes or until onion is translucent.

2. Add broth; bring to a boil. Stir in turkey, corn, tomatoes, rice mix and chipotle peppers. Reduce heat to low; cover and cook about 20 minutes or until rice is tender. Let stand 3 minutes. Sprinkle with green onion, if desired.

Makes 4 servings

Skillet Pasta Roma

½ pound Italian sausage, sliced or crumbled

1 large onion, coarsely chopped

1 large clove garlic, minced

2 cans (14.5 ounces each) DEL MONTE® Diced Tomatoes with Basil, Garlic & Oregano

1 can (8 ounces) DEL MONTE® Tomato Sauce

1 cup water

8 ounces uncooked rotini or other spiral pasta

8 mushrooms, sliced (optional)

Grated Parmesan cheese and fresh parsley sprigs (optional)

1. Brown sausage in large skillet. Add onion and garlic. Cook until onion is soft; drain. Stir in undrained tomatoes, tomato sauce, water and pasta.

2. Cover and bring to a boil; reduce heat. Simmer, covered, 25 to 30 minutes or until pasta is tender, stirring occasionally.

3. Stir in mushrooms, if desired; simmer 5 minutes. Serve in skillet garnished with cheese and parsley, if desired.

Makes 4 servings

ALL-IN-ONE BURGER STEW

1 pound ground beef

2 cups frozen Italian-style vegetables

1 can (about 14 ounces) diced tomatoes with basil and garlic

1 can (about 14 ounces) beef broth

2½ cups uncooked medium egg noodles

Salt and black pepper

1. Brown beef in large skillet over medium-high heat 6 to 8 minutes, stirring to break up meat. Drain fat.

2. Add vegetables, tomatoes and broth; bring to a boil over high heat.

3. Add noodles; cover and cook over medium heat 12 to 15 minutes or until vegetables and noodles are tender. Season with salt and pepper.

Makes 6 servings

QUICK-FIX
CASSEROLES

HAM ASPARAGUS GRATIN

1 can (10¾ ounces) CAMPBELL'S® Condensed Cream of Asparagus Soup

½ cup milk

¼ teaspoon onion powder

¼ teaspoon ground black pepper

1½ cups cooked cut asparagus

1½ cups cubed cooked ham

2¼ cups corkscrew-shaped pasta (rotini), cooked and drained

1 cup shredded Cheddar cheese **or** Swiss cheese (about 4 ounces)

1. Stir the soup, milk, onion powder, black pepper, asparagus, ham, pasta and ½ **cup** cheese in a 2-quart shallow baking dish.

2. Bake at 400°F. for 25 minutes or until the ham mixture is hot and bubbling. Stir the ham mixture. Sprinkle with the remaining cheese.

3. Bake for 5 minutes or until the cheese is melted.

Makes 4 servings

Hearty Potato and Sausage Bake

1 pound new red potatoes, cut into halves or quarters

1 onion, sliced

8 ounces carrots, cut into 3-inch sticks or baby carrots

2 tablespoons butter, melted

1 teaspoon salt

1 teaspoon garlic powder

½ teaspoon dried thyme

½ teaspoon black pepper

1 pound cooked chicken sausage or turkey sausage, cut into ¼-inch slices

1. Preheat oven to 400°F. Spray 13×9-inch baking dish with nonstick cooking spray.

2. Combine potatoes, onion, carrots, butter, salt, garlic powder, thyme and pepper in prepared baking dish; toss to coat.

3. Bake 30 minutes. Add sausage; mix well. Bake 15 to 20 minutes or until potatoes are tender and golden brown.

Makes 4 to 6 servings

Beef in Wine Sauce

4 pounds boneless beef chuck roast, cut into
1½- to 2-inch cubes

2 cans (10¾ ounces each) condensed golden mushroom
soup, undiluted

1 can (8 ounces) sliced mushrooms, drained

¾ cup dry sherry

2 tablespoons garlic powder

1 package (1 ounce) dry onion soup mix

1 bag (20 ounces) frozen sliced carrots, thawed

1. Preheat oven to 325°F. Spray 4-quart casserole with nonstick cooking spray.

2. Combine beef, soup, mushrooms, sherry, garlic powder and dry soup mix in prepared casserole; mix well.

3. Cover and bake 3 hours or until beef is tender. Add carrots during last 15 minutes of cooking.

Makes 6 to 8 servings

BAKED HALIBUT CASSEROLE

4 fresh or thawed frozen halibut steaks (1 inch thick, about 6 ounces each), rinsed

Salt and black pepper

1 can (8 ounces) tomato sauce

1 package (12 ounces) frozen mixed vegetables such as broccoli, peas, onions and bell peppers

Hot cooked rice (optional)

1. Preheat oven to 350°F. Rinse halibut and place in 13×9-inch baking pan. Season with salt and pepper.

2. Top with tomato sauce and vegetables; season with salt and pepper.

3. Bake 25 to 30 minutes or until fish begins to flake when tested with fork. Serve over rice, if desired.

Makes 4 servings

E-Z Chicken Tortilla Bake

1 can (10¾ ounces) condensed tomato soup, undiluted

1 cup ORTEGA® Thick & Chunky Salsa

½ cup milk

2 cups cubed cooked chicken

8 (8-inch) ORTEGA® Flour Soft Tortillas, cut into
   1-inch pieces

1 cup (4 ounces) shredded Cheddar cheese, divided

PREHEAT the oven to 400°F. Mix soup, salsa, milk, chicken, tortillas and ½ cup cheese in 2-quart shallow baking dish. Cover; bake 30 minutes or until hot. Top with remaining ½ cup cheese.

Makes 4 servings

TIP: Use turkey instead of chicken for an E-Z Turkey Tortilla Bake.

TIP: Two whole chicken breasts (about 10 ounces each) will yield about 2 cups of chopped cooked chicken.

PREP TIME: 10 minutes
START TO FINISH TIME: 40 minutes

CREAMY SHRIMP AND VEGETABLE CASSEROLE

1 pound fresh or thawed frozen shrimp, peeled and deveined

1 can (10¾ ounces) condensed cream of celery soup, undiluted

½ cup sliced fresh or thawed frozen asparagus (1-inch pieces)

½ cup sliced mushrooms

¼ cup diced red bell pepper

¼ cup sliced green onions

1 clove garlic, minced

¾ teaspoon dried thyme

¼ teaspoon black pepper

Hot cooked rice or orzo (optional)

1. Preheat oven to 375°F. Spray 2-quart baking dish with nonstick cooking spray.

2. Combine shrimp, soup, asparagus, mushrooms, bell pepper, green onions, garlic, thyme and black pepper in prepared baking dish.

3. Cover and bake 30 minutes. Serve over rice, if desired.

Makes 4 servings

ONE-POT
WONDERS

SHRIMP AND PEPPER NOODLE BOWL

- 4 cups water
- 2 packages (3 ounces each) shrimp-flavored ramen noodles
- 8 ounces frozen cooked medium shrimp *or* 1 package (8 ounces) frozen cooked baby shrimp
- 1 cup bell pepper strips
- ¼ cup chopped green onions
- 1 tablespoon soy sauce
- ½ teaspoon hot pepper sauce
- 2 tablespoons chopped fresh cilantro (optional)

1. Bring water to a boil in large saucepan over high heat. Remove seasoning packets from noodles. Break up noodles; add to boiling water. Add shrimp and bell pepper; cook 3 minutes.

2. Stir in seasoning packets, green onions, soy sauce and hot pepper sauce; cook 1 minute. Sprinkle with cilantro, if desired.

Makes 4 servings

Chicken Florentine in Minutes

3 cups water

1 cup milk

2 tablespoons butter

2 packages (about 4 ounces each) fettuccine Alfredo or stroganoff pasta mix

¼ teaspoon black pepper

1 package (about 10 ounces) refrigerated fully cooked chicken breast strips, cut into ½-inch pieces

4 cups baby spinach, coarsely chopped

¼ cup diced roasted red pepper

¼ cup sour cream

1. Combine water, milk and butter in large saucepan; bring to a boil over medium-high heat. Stir in pasta mix and black pepper. Reduce heat to medium; cook and stir 8 minutes or until pasta is tender.

2. Stir in chicken, spinach and roasted pepper; cook 2 minutes or until heated through.

3. Remove from heat; stir in sour cream.

Makes 4 servings

Italian Sausage and Vegetable Stew

1 pound hot or mild Italian sausage links, cut into 1-inch pieces

1 package (16 ounces) frozen vegetable blend, such as onions and bell peppers

2 medium zucchini, sliced

1 can (about 14 ounces) Italian-style diced tomatoes

1 can (4 ounces) sliced mushrooms, drained

4 cloves garlic, minced

1. Brown sausage in large saucepan over medium-high heat 5 minutes, stirring frequently. Drain fat.

2. Add frozen vegetables, zucchini, tomatoes, mushrooms and garlic; bring to a boil. Reduce heat to medium-low; cover and simmer 10 minutes. Uncover; cook 5 to 10 minutes or until thickened slightly.

Makes 6 servings

BOWTIE PASTA BOWL

    3 cups reduced-sodium chicken broth
    6 ounces uncooked bowtie pasta
    ⅛ teaspoon red pepper flakes
1½ cups diced cooked chicken
    1 medium tomato, seeded and diced
    1 cup packed spring greens or fresh spinach,
        coarsely chopped
    3 tablespoons chopped fresh basil
    ½ teaspoon salt
    1 cup (4 ounces) shredded mozzarella cheese
    2 tablespoons grated Parmesan cheese

1. Bring broth to boil in large saucepan over high heat. Add pasta and red pepper flakes; return to a boil. Reduce heat to medium-low; cover and simmer 10 minutes or until pasta is tender.

2. Add chicken; cook 1 minute. Remove from heat; stir in tomato, greens, basil and salt.

3. Top with mozzarella and Parmesan.

Makes 4 servings

CONFETTI CHICKEN CHILI

2 teaspoons olive oil

1 pound ground chicken or turkey

1 large onion, chopped

3½ cups reduced-sodium chicken broth

1 can (about 15 ounces) Great Northern beans, rinsed and drained

2 carrots, chopped

1 medium green bell pepper, chopped

2 plum tomatoes, chopped

1 jalapeño pepper,* finely chopped (optional)

2 teaspoons chili powder

½ teaspoon ground red pepper

*Jalapeño peppers can sting and irritate the skin, so wear rubber gloves when handling peppers and do not touch your eyes.

1. Heat oil in large saucepan over medium heat. Add chicken and onion; cook and stir 5 minutes or until chicken is browned. Drain fat.

2. Stir in broth, beans, carrots, bell pepper, tomatoes, jalapeño, if desired, chili powder and red pepper; bring to a boil over high heat. Reduce heat to low; cover and simmer 15 minutes.

Makes 4 servings

SLOW-COOKER
SUPPERS

SLOW COOKER SOUTHWESTERN PORK ROAST

2½ pounds boneless pork roast

1 envelope LIPTON® RECIPE SECRETS® Onion Soup Mix

1 can (14½ ounces) diced tomatoes, undrained

2 cans (4 ounces each) chopped green chilies, undrained

3 tablespoons firmly packed brown sugar

2 teaspoons chili powder

1 teaspoon ground cumin

1. In slow cooker, arrange pork. Combine soup mix with remaining ingredients; pour over pork.

2. Cook, covered, on low 8 to 10 hours or on high 4 to 6 hours or until pork is tender. Serve, if desired, with hot cooked rice or noodles.

Makes 8 servings

PREP TIME: 5 minutes
COOK TIME: 4 hours (High)

Nice 'n' Easy Italian Chicken

- 4 boneless skinless chicken breasts (about 4 ounces each)
- 8 ounces mushrooms, sliced
- 1 medium green bell pepper, chopped
- 1 medium zucchini, diced
- 1 medium onion, chopped
- 1 jar (26 ounces) pasta sauce
  Hot cooked pasta (optional)

1. Combine chicken, mushrooms, bell pepper, zucchini, onion and pasta sauce in slow cooker.

2. Cover; cook on LOW 6 to 8 hours or until chicken is tender. Serve over pasta, if desired.

Makes 4 servings

THREE-BEAN MOLE CHILI

1 can (about 15 ounces) chili beans in spicy sauce

1 can (about 15 ounces) pinto beans, rinsed and drained

1 can (about 15 ounces) black beans, rinsed and drained

1 can (about 14 ounces) Mexican- or chili-style diced tomatoes

1 large green bell pepper, diced

1 small onion, diced

½ cup beef, chicken or vegetable broth

¼ cup prepared mole paste*

2 teaspoons ground cumin

2 teaspoons chili powder

2 teaspoons ground coriander (optional)

2 teaspoons minced garlic

Toppings: crushed tortilla chips, chopped cilantro or shredded cheese

Mole paste is available in the Mexican aisle of large supermarkets or in specialty markets.

1. Combine beans, tomatoes, bell pepper, onion, broth, mole paste, cumin, chili powder, coriander, if desired, and garlic in slow cooker.

2. Cover; cook on LOW 5 to 6 hours. Serve with desired toppings.

Makes 4 to 6 servings

CARIBBEAN SWEET POTATO AND BEAN STEW

2 medium sweet potatoes (about 1 pound), peeled and cut into 1-inch cubes

2 cups frozen cut green beans

1 can (about 15 ounces) black beans, rinsed and drained

1 can (about 14 ounces) vegetable broth

1 small onion, sliced

2 teaspoons Caribbean jerk seasoning

½ teaspoon dried thyme

¼ teaspoon salt

¼ teaspoon ground cinnamon

⅓ cup slivered almonds, toasted*

Hot pepper sauce (optional)

To toast almonds, cook in heavy skillet over medium heat 1 to 2 minutes or until nuts are lightly browned, stirring frequently.

1. Combine sweet potatoes, green beans, black beans, broth, onion, jerk seasoning, thyme, salt and cinnamon in slow cooker.

2. Cover; cook on LOW 5 to 6 hours or until vegetables are tender. Serve with almonds and hot pepper sauce, if desired.

Makes 4 servings

Beef Bourguignonne

1   can (10¾ ounces) CAMPBELL'S® Condensed
    Golden Mushroom Soup

1   cup Burgundy **or** other dry red wine

2   cloves garlic, minced

1   teaspoon dried thyme leaves, crushed

2   cups small button mushrooms (about 6 ounces)

2   cups fresh **or** thawed frozen baby carrots

1   cup frozen small whole onions, thawed

1½ pounds beef top round steak, 1½-inches thick,
    cut into 1-inch pieces

1. Stir the soup, wine, garlic, thyme, mushrooms, carrots,
onions and beef in a 3½-quart slow cooker.

2. Cover and cook on LOW for 8 to 9 hours* or until the
beef is fork-tender.

Or on HIGH for 4 to 5 hours.

Makes 6 servings

PREP TIME: 10 minutes
COOK TIME: 8 hours

No-Fuss Macaroni and Cheese

- 2 cups (about 8 ounces) uncooked elbow macaroni
- 4 ounces pasteurized process cheese product, cubed
- 1 cup (4 ounces) shredded Cheddar cheese
- ½ teaspoon salt
- ⅛ teaspoon black pepper
- 1½ cups milk

1. Combine macaroni, cheese product, Cheddar, salt and pepper in slow cooker. Pour milk over top.

2. Cover; cook on LOW 2 to 3 hours, stirring after 20 to 30 minutes.

Makes 6 to 8 servings

VARIATION: Stir in sliced hot dogs or vegetables near the end of cooking. Cover; cook until heated through.

NOTE: As with all macaroni and cheese dishes, the cheese sauce thickens and begins to dry out as it sits. If it becomes too dry, stir in a little extra milk. Do not cook longer than 4 hours.

CONTENTS

CLASSIC
DUMP CAKES

PEACH MELBA DUMP CAKE

- 2 cans (21 ounces each) peach pie filling
- 1 package (12 ounces) frozen raspberries, thawed and drained
- 1 package (about 15 ounces) yellow cake mix
- ½ cup (1 stick) butter, cut into thin slices
  Ice cream (optional)

1. Preheat oven to 350°F. Spray 13×9-inch baking pan with nonstick cooking spray.

2. Spread peach pie filling in prepared pan; sprinkle with raspberries. Top with cake mix, spreading evenly. Top with butter in single layer, covering cake mix as much as possible.

3. Bake 40 to 45 minutes or until toothpick inserted into center of cake comes out clean. Cool at least 15 minutes before serving. Serve with ice cream, if desired.

Makes 12 to 16 servings

DOUBLE PINEAPPLE BERRY CAKE

1 can (20 ounces) crushed pineapple, undrained

1 package (12 ounces) frozen mixed berries, thawed and drained

1 package (about 18 ounces) pineapple cake mix

½ cup (1 stick) butter, cut into thin slices

Whipped cream (optional)

1. Preheat oven to 350°F. Spray 13×9-inch baking pan with nonstick cooking spray.

2. Spread pineapple and berries in prepared pan. Top with cake mix, spreading evenly. Top with butter in single layer, covering cake mix as much as possible.

3. Bake 45 to 50 minutes or until toothpick inserted into center of cake comes out clean. Cool at least 15 minutes before serving. Serve with whipped cream, if desired.

Makes 12 to 16 servings

Simple S'more Cake

- 1 package (about 15 ounces) milk chocolate cake mix
- 1 package (4-serving size) chocolate instant pudding and pie filling mix
- 1½ cups milk
- 1 cup mini marshmallows
- 3 bars (1.55 ounces each) milk chocolate bars, broken into pieces *or* 1 cup milk chocolate chips
- 3 whole graham crackers, broken into bite-size pieces

1. Preheat oven to 350°F. Spray 13×9-inch baking pan with nonstick cooking spray.

2. Combine cake mix, pudding mix and milk in large bowl; beat 1 to 2 minutes or until well blended. Spread batter in prepared pan.

3. Bake 30 to 35 minutes or until toothpick inserted into center comes out clean. *Turn oven to broil.*

4. Sprinkle marshmallows, chocolate and graham crackers over cake. Broil 6 inches from heat source 30 seconds to 1 minute or until marshmallows are golden brown. (Watch carefully to prevent burning.) Cool at least 5 minutes before serving.

Makes 12 to 16 servings

BANANA SPLIT CAKE

- 1 can (20 ounces) crushed pineapple, undrained
- 1 can (14½ ounces) tart cherries in water, drained
- 1 package (about 18 ounces) banana cake mix
- ½ cup (1 stick) butter, cut into thin slices
- ½ cup semisweet chocolate chips
- ½ cup chopped pecans
  Whipped cream and maraschino cherries (optional)

1. Preheat oven to 350°F. Spray 13×9-inch baking pan with nonstick cooking spray.

2. Spread pineapple and cherries in prepared pan. Top with cake mix, spreading evenly. Top with butter in single layer, covering cake mix as much as possible. Sprinkle with chocolate chips and pecans.

3. Bake 55 to 60 minutes or until toothpick inserted into center of cake comes out clean. Cool at least 15 minutes before serving. Top with whipped cream and cherries, if desired.

Makes 12 to 16 servings

Mixed Berry Dump Cake

2 packages (12 ounces each) frozen mixed berries, thawed and drained

1 package (about 15 ounces) white cake mix

¼ teaspoon ground cinnamon

1 can (12 ounces) lemon-lime soda

½ cup cinnamon chips

1. Preheat oven to 350°F. Spray 13×9-inch baking pan with nonstick cooking spray.

2. Spread berries in prepared pan. Top with cake mix, spreading evenly. Sprinkle with cinnamon. Slowly pour soda over top, covering cake mix as much as possible. Sprinkle with cinnamon chips.

3. Bake 45 to 50 minutes or until toothpick inserted into center of cake comes out clean. Cool at least 15 minutes before serving.

Makes 12 to 16 servings

Cha-Cha-Cha Cherry Cake

2 packages (12 ounces each) frozen cherries,
    thawed and drained

1 package (4-serving size) cherry gelatin

1 package (about 15 ounces) white cake mix

½ cup (1 stick) butter, cut into thin slices

1 cup chopped walnuts

¼ cup water

1. Preheat oven to 350°F. Spray 9-inch square baking pan with nonstick cooking spray.

2. Spread cherries in prepared pan; sprinkle with gelatin. Top with cake mix, spreading evenly. Top with butter in single layer, covering cake mix as much as possible. Sprinkle with walnuts. Drizzle water over top.

3. Bake 50 to 60 minutes or until toothpick inserted into center of cake comes out clean. Cool at least 15 minutes before serving.

Makes 9 servings

TROPICAL DUMP CAKE

1 can (20 ounces) crushed pineapple, undrained
1 can (15 ounces) peach slices in light syrup, undrained
1 package (about 15 ounces) yellow cake mix
½ cup (1 stick) butter, cut into thin slices
1 cup packed brown sugar
½ cup flaked coconut
½ cup chopped pecans

1. Preheat oven to 350°F. Spray 13×9-inch pan with nonstick cooking spray.

2. Spread pineapple and peaches in prepared pan. Top with cake mix, spreading evenly. Top with butter in single layer, covering cake mix as much as possible. Sprinkle with brown sugar, coconut and pecans.

3. Bake 40 to 45 minutes or until toothpick inserted into center of cake comes out clean. Cool at least 15 minutes before serving.

Makes 12 to 16 servings

BLUEBERRY CINNAMON CAKE

2 packages (12 ounces each) frozen blueberries, thawed and drained *or* 4½ cups fresh blueberries

⅓ cup sugar

¾ teaspoon ground cinnamon, divided

1 package (about 15 ounces) yellow cake mix

¾ cup (1½ sticks) butter, cut into thin slices

Ice cream (optional)

1. Preheat oven to 350°F. Spray 13×9-inch baking pan with nonstick cooking spray.

2. Spread blueberries in prepared pan. Sprinkle with sugar and ½ teaspoon cinnamon; toss to coat. Top with cake mix, spreading evenly. Top with butter in single layer, covering cake mix as much as possible. Sprinkle with remaining ¼ teaspoon cinnamon.

3. Bake 50 to 60 minutes or until toothpick inserted into center of cake comes out clean. Cool at least 15 minutes before serving. Serve with ice cream, if desired.

Makes 12 to 16 servings

FAMILY
FAVORITES

CHERRY CHEESECAKE DUMP CAKE

- 1 can (21 ounces) cherry pie filling
- 1 can (14½ ounces) tart cherries in water, drained
- 4 ounces cream cheese, cut into small pieces
- 1 package (about 15 ounces) yellow cake mix
- ½ cup (1 stick) butter, cut into thin slices

1. Preheat oven to 350°F. Spray 13×9-inch baking pan with nonstick cooking spray.

2. Spread cherry pie filling and cherries in prepared pan. Scatter cream cheese pieces over cherries. Top with cake mix, spreading evenly. Top with butter in single layer, covering cake mix as much as possible.

3. Bake 45 to 50 minutes or until toothpick inserted into center of cake comes out clean. Cool at least 15 minutes before serving.

Makes 12 to 16 servings

APRICOT DOUBLE CHIP CAKE

- 2 cups apricot preserves or jam
- ½ cup semisweet chocolate chips, divided
- ½ cup white chocolate chips, divided
- 1 package (about 15 ounces) yellow cake mix
- ½ cup (1 stick) butter, cut into thin slices
- ⅓ cup water

1. Preheat oven to 350°F. Spray 9-inch square baking pan with nonstick cooking spray.

2. Spread preserves in prepared pan. Sprinkle with half of semisweet chips and half of white chips. Top with cake mix, spreading evenly. Top with butter in single layer, covering cake mix as much as possible. Drizzle water over top. Sprinkle with remaining semisweet and white chips.

3. Bake 50 to 55 minutes or until toothpick inserted into center of cake comes out clean. Cool at least 15 minutes before serving.

Makes 9 servings

Red Velvet White Chip Cake

- 1 package (about 18 ounces) red velvet cake mix
- 1 package (4-serving size) vanilla instant pudding and pie filling mix
- 1½ cups milk
- 2 ounces cream cheese, cut into small pieces
- ½ cup white chocolate chips

1. Preheat oven to 350°F. Spray 13×9-inch baking pan with nonstick cooking spray.

2. Combine cake mix, pudding mix and milk in large bowl; beat until well blended. Spread batter in prepared pan; sprinkle with cream cheese pieces and white chips.

3. Bake 25 to 30 minutes or until toothpick inserted into center comes out clean. Cool in pan on wire rack. Serve warm or at room temperature.

Makes 12 to 16 servings

Raspberry Lovers' Dump Cake

1 can (21 ounces) raspberry pie filling

1 package (12 ounces) frozen raspberries, thawed and drained

1 package (12 ounces) semisweet chocolate chips, divided

1 package (about 15 ounces) white cake mix

¾ cup (1½ sticks) butter, cut into thin slices

½ cup packed brown sugar

Ice cream (optional)

1. Preheat oven to 350°F. Spray 13×9-inch baking pan with nonstick cooking spray.

2. Spread raspberry pie filling in prepared pan; sprinkle with raspberries. Sprinkle with half of chocolate chips. Top with cake mix, spreading evenly. Top with butter in single layer, covering cake mix as much as possible. Sprinkle with brown sugar and remaining chocolate chips.

3. Bake 50 to 60 minutes or until golden brown and toothpick inserted into center of cake comes out clean. Cool at least 15 minutes before serving. Serve with ice cream, if desired.

Makes 12 to 16 servings

BLACKBERRY ALMOND CAKE

2 packages (12 ounces each) frozen blackberries, thawed and drained

¼ cup granulated sugar

1 package (about 15 ounces) yellow cake mix

¾ cup (1½ sticks) butter, cut into thin slices

½ cup sliced almonds

¼ cup packed brown sugar

1. Preheat oven to 350°F. Spray 13×9-inch baking pan with nonstick cooking spray.

2. Spread blackberries in prepared pan; sprinkle with granulated sugar and toss to coat. Top with cake mix, spreading evenly. Top with butter in single layer, covering cake mix as much as possible. Sprinkle with almonds and brown sugar.

3. Bake 50 to 60 minutes or until toothpick inserted into center of cake comes out clean. Cool at least 15 minutes before serving.

Makes 12 to 16 servings

ISLAND DELIGHT CAKE

3 ripe mangoes, peeled and cubed (about 4½ cups)

1 package (about 18 ounces) pineapple cake mix

1 can (12 ounces) lemon-lime or orange soda

½ cup chopped macadamia nuts (optional)

1. Preheat oven to 350°F. Spray 13×9-inch baking pan with nonstick cooking spray.

2. Spread mangoes in prepared pan. Top with cake mix, spreading evenly. Pour soda over top, covering cake mix as much as possible. Sprinkle with macadamia nuts, if desired.

3. Bake 35 to 40 minutes or until toothpick inserted into center of cake comes out clean. Cool at least 15 minutes before serving.

Makes 12 to 16 servings

Rainbow Dump Cake

1 can (20 ounces) crushed pineapple, undrained
1 can (14½ ounces) tart cherries in water, drained
1 package (about 15 ounces) yellow cake mix
½ cup (1 stick) butter, cut into thin slices
½ cup candy-coated chocolate pieces

1. Preheat oven to 350°F. Spray 13×9-inch baking pan with nonstick cooking spray.

2. Spread pineapple and cherries in prepared pan. Top with cake mix, spreading evenly. Top with butter in single layer, covering cake mix as much as possible.

3. Bake 35 to 40 minutes or until toothpick inserted into center of cake comes out clean, sprinkling with chocolate pieces during last 10 minutes of baking. Cool at least 15 minutes before serving.

Makes 12 to 16 servings

FALL
FLAVORS

CRANBERRY APPLE CAKE

1   can (21 ounces) apple pie filling
1   can (14 ounces) whole berry cranberry sauce
1   package (about 15 ounces) yellow cake mix
½   cup (1 stick) butter, cut into thin slices
½   cup chopped walnuts

1. Preheat oven to 350°F. Spray 13×9-inch baking pan with nonstick cooking spray.

2. Spread apple pie filling in prepared pan; top with cranberry sauce. Top with cake mix, spreading evenly. Top with butter in single layer, covering cake mix as much as possible. Sprinkle with walnuts.

3. Bake 50 to 55 minutes or until toothpick inserted into center of cake comes out clean. Cool at least 15 minutes before serving.

Makes 12 to 16 servings

PUMPKIN PECAN CAKE

1 can (15 ounces) solid-pack pumpkin

1 can (12 ounces) evaporated milk

1 cup packed brown sugar

3 eggs

2 teaspoons pumpkin pie spice

½ teaspoon salt

1 package (about 15 ounces) yellow cake mix

¾ cup (1½ sticks) butter, cut into thin slices

½ cup pecan halves

1. Preheat oven to 350°F. Spray 13×9-inch baking pan with nonstick cooking spray.

2. Combine pumpkin, evaporated milk, brown sugar, eggs, pumpkin pie spice and salt in medium bowl; stir until well blended. Pour into prepared pan; top with cake mix, spreading evenly. Top with butter in single layer, covering cake mix as much as possible. Sprinkle with pecans.

3. Bake about 1 hour or until toothpick inserted into center of cake comes out clean. Cool completely in pan on wire rack.

Makes 12 to 16 servings

GRANOLA CARAMEL CARROT CAKE

1 can (20 ounces) crushed pineapple, undrained
1 package (about 15 ounces) carrot cake mix
½ cup (1 stick) butter, cut into thin slices
1 cup granola
3 tablespoons caramel topping, warmed
Ice cream (optional)

1. Preheat oven to 350°F. Spray 13×9-inch baking pan with nonstick cooking spray.

2. Spread pineapple in prepared pan. Top with cake mix, spreading evenly. Top with butter in single layer, covering cake mix as much as possible. Sprinkle with granola; drizzle with caramel topping.

3. Bake 50 to 55 minutes or until toothpick inserted into center of cake comes out clean. Cool at least 15 minutes before serving. Serve with ice cream, if desired.

Makes 12 to 16 servings

Sweet Potato Cake

1 can (29 ounces) sweet potatoes in light syrup, drained
1 package (about 15 ounces) yellow cake mix
3 eggs
1½ teaspoons apple pie spice, plus additional for top of cake
⅔ cup chopped nuts, divided

1. Preheat oven to 350°F. Spray 13×9-inch baking pan with nonstick cooking spray.

2. Place sweet potatoes in large bowl; mash with fork. Add cake mix, eggs and 1½ teaspoons apple pie spice; beat 1 to 2 minutes or until well blended. Stir in ⅓ cup nuts. Spread batter in prepared pan; sprinkle with remaining ⅓ cup nuts and additional apple pie spice.

3. Bake 30 to 35 minutes or until toothpick inserted into center comes out clean. Cool in pan at least 15 minutes before serving.

Makes 12 to 16 servings

ORANGE CRANBERRY CAKE

1 package (about 15 ounces) yellow cake mix

4 eggs

¾ cup orange juice

½ cup canola or vegetable oil

¼ cup water

1 cup dried cranberries

Powdered sugar (optional)

1. Preheat oven to 350°F. Grease and flour 12-cup (10-inch) bundt pan.

2. Combine cake mix, eggs, orange juice, oil and water in large bowl; beat 1 to 2 minutes or until well blended. Stir in cranberries. Pour batter into prepared pan.

3. Bake about 40 minutes or until toothpick inserted near center comes out clean. Cool in pan 10 minutes; invert onto wire rack to cool completely. Sprinkle with powdered sugar, if desired.

Makes 12 servings

CARAMEL APPLE PEANUT CAKE

2 cans (21 ounces each) apple pie filling

½ cup lightly salted peanuts, divided

1 package (about 15 ounces) yellow cake mix

½ cup (1 stick) butter, cut into thin slices

⅓ cup caramel topping, heated

1. Preheat oven to 350°F. Spray 13×9-inch baking pan with nonstick cooking spray.

2. Spread apple pie filling in prepared pan; sprinkle with ¼ cup peanuts. Top with cake mix, spreading evenly. Top with butter in single layer, covering cake mix as much as possible. Drizzle with caramel topping; sprinkle with remaining ¼ cup peanuts.

3. Bake 35 to 40 minutes or until toothpick inserted into center of cake comes out clean. Cool at least 15 minutes before serving.

Makes 12 to 16 servings

Autumn Dump Cake

1 can (29 ounces) pear pieces in light syrup, undrained
1 can (21 ounces) apple pie filling
½ cup dried cranberries
1 package (about 15 ounces) yellow cake mix
½ cup (1 stick) butter, cut into thin slices
¼ cup caramel topping, warmed

1. Preheat oven to 350°F. Spray 13×9-inch baking pan with nonstick cooking spray.

2. Drain pears, reserving ½ cup syrup. Spread pears and apple pie filling in prepared pan; drizzle with reserved pear syrup. Sprinkle with cranberries. Top with cake mix, spreading evenly. Top with butter in single layer, covering cake mix as much as possible. Drizzle with caramel topping.

3. Bake 40 to 45 minutes or until toothpick inserted into center of cake comes out clean. Cool at least 15 minutes before serving.

Makes 12 to 16 servings

Pumpkin Chocolate Chip Cake

1 package (about 15 ounces) spice cake mix
1 can (15 ounces) solid-pack pumpkin
2 eggs
⅓ cup water
1 cup semisweet chocolate chips
1 cup semisweet chocolate chips, melted (optional)

1. Preheat oven to 350°F. Grease and flour 12-cup (10-inch) bundt pan.

2. Combine cake mix, pumpkin, eggs and water in large bowl; beat 1 to 2 minutes or until well blended. Stir in 1 cup chocolate chips. Spread batter in prepared pan.

3. Bake 35 to 40 minutes or until toothpick inserted near center comes out clean. Cool in pan 10 minutes; invert onto wire rack to cool completely.

4. Drizzle melted chocolate over cooled cake, if desired.

Makes 12 servings

ACKNOWLEDGMENTS

The publisher would like to thank the companies listed below for the use of their recipes and photographs in this publication.

Campbell Soup Company

Del Monte Foods

Ortega®, A Division of B&G Foods North America, Inc.

Reckitt Benckiser LLC.

Unilever